The Quiet Corner

FREDERICK MULLER LIMITED
LONDON

COLOUR GIFT BOOKS

Perfect gift books at little more than the cost of a greeting card. A completely new series illustrated throughout in *superb full colour.* Each 32 pages.

LOOKING FORWARD
BESIDE THE STILL WATERS
LIGHT FOR TODAY
THOUGHTS GO HOME
TAKE COMFORT
NATURE'S CATHEDRAL
THE RHYTHM OF THE SEASONS
RING IN THE NEW

THE GLORY BEYOND
GIVE LIFE TIME
THE HARBOUR OF CONTENTMENT
QUIET THOUGHTS FOR THE QUIET HOUR
THE LAMP OF CHEERFULNESS
THE GARDEN THROUGH THE YEAR
OUT INTO THE SUNSHINE
THE HAVEN OF THE HEART

THE QUIET HOUR Series

HOUSE OF DREAMS
SOMEWHERE OVER THE HILL
THE BEST IS YET TO COME
COME HAPPY DAY
WINGS OF THE MORNING
THROUGH THE YEAR

THE QUIET CORNER
THE QUIET HOUR
QUIET MOMENTS
ROSES FOR REMEMBRANCE
PASSING CLOUDS
HARBOURS OF HAPPINESS

ILLUSTRATED GIFT BOOKS

GIVE ME A QUIET CORNER

Based on Patience Strong's own philosophy of life, offering thoughts of hope, contentment and faith. These verses with their evocative accompanying photographs make this book one that every admirer will turn to for inspiration in time of need.

THE HARVEST OF A QUIET EYE
THE TAPESTRY OF TIME
HOMES AND GARDENS

DAILY READINGS

THE BIRTHDAY BOOK
THE BEDSIDE BOOK
THE FRIENDSHIP BOOK
THE MORNING WATCH
THE GLORY OF THE GARDEN
THE GIFT BOOK
THE KINGDOM WITHIN

LIFE IS FOR LIVING

Patience Strong's study of practical psychology.

The Quiet Corner
Patience Strong

First published in Great Britain 1978
by Frederick Muller Limited, London, NW2 6LE

ISBN 0 584 10625 4

Colour Photographs by Colour Library International Ltd.
CLI House, Coombe Road, New Malden, Surrey.
Line drawings by Cara Lockhart Smith

Printed in Spain

The Quiet Corner
Patience Strong

Turn the Page

Life's a book in which we write the story of the years.
If the one that's ending has been marked with clouds
and tears — Turn the leaf and on the fresh new page
that now you see — In golden letters write these
words: The best is yet to be.

The Heath

Nature will not tolerate the common-place, the plain,
the bare. She sets to work with paint and brush to add
some colour here and there.
This heath was once a wilderness of bush and bracken,
rough and coarse ... But now it blooms in golden glory
with the beauty of the gorse.

Clova Glen and Grampians, Angus, Scotland

In My Garden

O'er the wall the lilac blossoms fall in white and purple
showers. On the lawn the slim laburnum spreads its
honey-coloured flowers.

Yellow, flame and gold and orange burn the bushes of
the broom — where along the garden path they flaunt
the glory of their bloom.

Hawthorns snowy, pink and crimson — toss their petal:
far and wide — Just as if they threw confetti for the
passing of a bride.

Laburnum

Tongues of Fire

At Whitsuntide the world recalls that strange
mysterious hour — when men, touched by the Holy
Ghost, received new strength and power. Lord, quicken
and endow our spirits with the gifts of grace.
Pour the wine of inspiration into every place.
Send a Pentecostal wind to fan the soul's desire
—Warm the heart with Love that we may speak with
tongues of fire.

Aberdeen, Aberdeenshire, Scotland

God Willing

We planned our castles in the blue — We faced the
future unafraid. But where now is that happy world?
Where now the golden dreams we made?
Beneath the wreckage of lost hopes — the dust and
debris of the past ... But Love can never be destroyed.
So wait my dearest; trust — hold fast. Love survives
though castles fall.
If faith and fortitude remain — no evil chance can cheat
our hopes. God willing, we shall build again.

Tantallon Castle, East Lothian, Scotland

Temptation

When you're at your lowest level — do not listen to the
devil, for it's then he's sure to try and catch your ear...
When your strength is giving out — he is bound to be
about — with suggestions of defeat and doubt and fear.
When things harass and upset you — he will do his best
to get you — to admit that you are beaten, and give
in... That's the time for saying "No". That's the time
for you to show — that you mean to keep on going —
And to win!

Chrysanthemums with Michaelmas Daisies

The Wonderful One

Have you found your Paradise — and happiness true
and supreme?   Have you discovered the friend of your
heart?   Or are you in love with a dream?
Take no fake or second best. Though sometimes a lone
road it seems. One day you'll turn round a corner and
meet — The Wonderful One of your dreams.

Doing the Job

Bring to your task, however great or humble — your
highest standards of efficiency ... This is no time to
argue or to grumble.
Do what you can — and do it willingly. Stick to the job.
Take pride in it and pleasure. Give of your best. Flag not,
nor lag behind ... Stern are the times, demanding a full
measure — of your endurance; hand and heart and
mind.

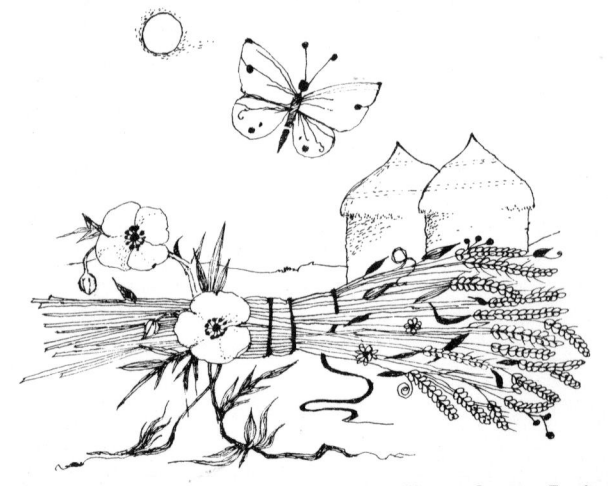

Horne, Surrey, England

The Good Angel

A good angel watches o'er those whom we love — We
must believe this is true — Or how could we bear to be
parted from them — For more than a moment or two?
This is the faith that we hold in the heart — stronger
and deeper than fear; the knowledge that one of God's
angels is there — to guard them when danger is near.

Daffodils and Primula

War Memorial

On market squares and village greens — unnumbered
war memorials stand — to speak for those who fought
and fell — and gave their all for this dear land.
With tongues of granite and of stone — they cry at us
accusingly, "Is this the world we won for you?   Did we
not die to make you free? "

King's College, Cambridge, Cambridgeshire, England

How Much do You Remember?

How much do you remember? How much do you
recall? Perhaps you have forgotten — but I remember
all; that day at Kew in April; the Spring bloom all
a-blow; that café on the corner of a street in old Soho.
The day we went to Putney to cheer the Oxford crew;
the day we spent in Surrey when all the woods were
blue... The first night at the Lyric. The last time that we
met. How much do you remember? How much do you
forget?

Broadwater Lake, Godalming, Surrey, England

Light in the West

While in the West the light still shines — We hold the dying day . . . The darkness cannot fall until the last gleam fades away.
While there is courage in the heart — We climb the highest hill... Disasters cannot crush the soul — nor failures break the will.

Clyde River, Glasgow, Lanarkshire, Scotland

The Last Dance

When the yellow leaves are falling from the tattered
trees — they seem to dance a measure to the music of
the breeze... Twirling, swirling, whirling wildly up and
down the lane; you hear the swishing of their skirts
against the window pane.
The last gay frolic of the leaves; their last mad revelry;
the last fandango of delight; the final ecstasy...
Dancing at the doors of Winter as the year grows old —
Covering the grave of Summer with a cloth of gold.

Worcester Cathedral, Worcester, West Midlands, England

Pines Against the Sky

Pines against the golden sunset — lovely and serene —
Like a picture painted on a brightly gilded screen.
Pines against the western skyline in the evening hour.
Whence comes beauty such as this?   What is its magic
power?
It seems to take us out of Time into Eternity. Can it be
God showing us a glimpse of things to be?

Honolulu, One of the Hawaiian Islands

Here Where the Old Road Ends

Here at the place where the old road ends — Here is the place to make amends. Dropping old grudges — and casting aside — Grievances, feuds and petty pride. Here where the untrodden path begins — Asking forgiveness for our sins... Here on the spot where the new roads start — Here we should pause and search the heart.

Dove Dale, Derbyshire, England

The Forest Fairyland

When we walk through the forest on wintry days —
where the trees stand hung with tinselled rime — How
strange it is in those frosted aisles! Like a fairy scene in
a Pantomime.
Not a breath stirs the peace of that weird white world
— Not a sound breaks the silence as we go — Only a
wing in a frozen bush — and the crunch of a footstep
in the snow.

Nevadd Reservoir and Pen y Fan National Park, Powys, Wales

Have Faith

Have Faith — For Faith will carry us along the hardest
road. Have Faith and Faith will give us strength to bear
the heavy load... Faith in something greater than the
power of mortal man. Faith that midst the chaos God
is working out a Plan.
Have Faith that He will bring us through, though dark
and dire the way. Have Faith that He is leading us unto
a brighter day... Though beneath our burdens bent,
steep paths we must ascend — Have Faith that we are
making for some good and glorious end.

Oppstryn, Norway

Bid the People Pray

"And ye shall know that I am in the midst of Israel."
— *Joel 2.*
We are sick and weary with disasters and defeats.
Gather in the people from the fields and from the
streets... Bid them to the House of God to make their
common prayer. His covenants proclaim aloud; His
holy word declare.
We wrestle with Satanic powers. We fight the hordes
of hell. But are we not His servant nation? Modern
Israel.
   ... The armies of the living God are on the march
today. Let the Church lift up her voice and bid the
people pray!

Chester Cathedral, Chester, Merseyside

Downland

Who could guess the century?   It might be any year...
Time, it seems, in passing by — has left no footprint
here. The village with its narrow street; the church, the
pond, the mill... The ploughman on the furrowed
slope — the shepherd on the hill. Here the heart could
be content to let the world go by — where the downs
rise broad and green against the Sussex sky.

Bossington, Somerset, England

The Bow in the Cloud

"I do set my bow in the cloud and it shall be for a
token of a covenant between me and the earth." —
Genesis 9.13.
A covenant of mercy the Lord has made with man —
and when across the heavens we see the rainbow span
— we see in all its glory God's promise made anew.
We know the pledge is certain. We know the word is
true.
A flood of devastation engulfs the world today. The
tide of evil rises — and much is swept away. But call
upon God's mercy. Lift up your weary eyes — and you
will see a rainbow beyond the stormy skies.

Killin, Perthshire, Scotland

The End of the Road

Where is the end of the road, my friend? Is it far? No
man can say... But it's somewhere out there where
the sun comes up — with the promise of the day.
And it can't be measured in yards or miles — nor in
terms of days and years — But in strength, endurance
and sacrifice — in courage and toil and tears.
It may be over the farthest hill — or it may be just
round the bend... But wherever it is we shall march
right on — and we'll get there in the end.

40

New Chapel, Surrey, England

Spring Eternal

Pity all those lonely souls who face an empty chair.
The broken-hearted, the bereaved, the victims of
despair... with nothing left but recollections of the
days now gone. Time rolls by and changes come —
but memories live on. Courage, courage, breaking
heart! Be strong, be glad, be brave — Your dear one is
not sleeping in the silence of the grave... But freed
from Life's injustices, from fear and suffering — they
walk beside you in the joy of God's Eternal Spring.

Richmond Park, Surrey, England

Unhappy World

There are many invalids who lie on beds of pain —
some who know that they will never taste life's joys
again: The blind, the lame, the paralysed, the
nerve-racked and the weak. If we want to do some
good, we have not far to seek. There's always
someone yearning for a bit of sympathy. There's
always someone up against some dire calamity.
There's always someone suffering no matter where we
go. Unhappy world! perhaps — but it's the only one
we know.

Roses with Silver Birch

The Appointment

Do you remember our first appointment — under the
clock at eight? ... We were young — Life was fun —
and the world seemed fair. For the future was ours and
we hadn't a care — when we kept our first appointment
— Under the clock at eight.
We, like so many, are parted now — But dearest for you
I'll wait ... If we hold to our faith we'll come smiling
through — Our wonderful dreams will all come true —
And another appointment I'll keep with you — Under
the clock at eight.

Richmond Park, Surrey

The Witnesses

"The sea is His and He made it."
Men whose duties lie upon the waters of the sea —
behold God walking on the waves in might and
majesty...
Out beyond the grey horizons where the big winds
sweep — They see the wonders of His spirit moving on
the deep.
They who sail the sea in ships are not as other men —
They have witnessed marvels never told by tongue or
pen — In tide and tempest, calm and storm, and
lightning's flaming sword — They have known and
heard and seen the presence of the Lord.

48

Castlepoint, North Island, New Zealand

Sudden Death

Swiftly, without warning, snatched away before our
eyes! When we witness sudden death we come to
realise — How near we are to the Eternal — closer
than we know — Nearer than we dream each day as
on our way we go.
Knowing not how often we approach the Borderline —
Stumbling in our blindness on the edge of things divine
... Transient is human life, and frail the mortal bond.
But God is Love, and friends are waiting in the world
beyond.

Chrysanthemums with Sprays of Gypsophila and Asparagus Fern

Sun and Frost

Frost has breathed upon the garden with its cold and
bitter breath. The pregnant earth lies petrified beneath
the thick grey shroud of death. Winter-white the world
appears. One feels the chill of hope deferred. But
suddenly, the heart is startled by the fluting of a bird.
See the sun comes up triumphant! ... setting all the
east ablaze. Frozen branches drip and shimmer in the
warm life-giving rays... Every blade is gem encrusted.
Every twig is dew impearled. Sun and frost make all
things lovely ... Light and warmth transform the world.

Winter in Norway

The Golden Clock

The countryman with practised eye — looking up into
the sky — can tell the time from dawn to dark —
following the Sun's bright arc — from east to west: a
shining span —compassing the days of man. Brief
winter — widening... with the coming of the spring.
He needs no watch who year by year — has seen the
morning sun appear — and marked its course
throughout the day — until the evening shadows lay
long and dark across the land, for he can read and
understand — the golden clock that hangs on high.
The hours are written in the sky.

Stonehenge, Wiltshire, England

"He Died Climbing"

Somewhere near the summit of a snowswept
mountain-side — There's a stone that marks the spot
where some lone climber died... The grand and
thrilling story of a glorious ascent — is written in three
words upon a simple monument.
He did not reach the cloudy crag that crowned the
towering wall. He did not stand triumphant on the
highest peak of all. But though he failed to set his foot
upon the final height — He died in the supreme
endeavour... with the goal in sight.

Torridon and Ben Damph, Ross and Cromarty, Scotland

Hope Returns

From my window I can see — the stark bare branches
of a tree... It seems a dead and lifeless thing — Yet in
its boughs the thrushes sing — As if they felt within
the wood — the new sap rising, rich and good; the
fresh life flowing secretly — from the deep roots of the
tree. I too — beneath my sombre mood — can feel the
surge of gratitude... From hidden depths of grief and
pain — God speaks ... And hope returns again.

Glen Affric, Inverness-shire, Scotland

Brightest and Best

Remember the good things, forgetting the bad — Cling
to the thought of the blessings you've had — Thankful
for everything precious and dear — Cherished
possessions, and friendships sincere.
Think of Life's beauties — and not of its pains. Much
has been taken — but much still remains... Remember
the fair days, forgetting the rest. Grateful for all that is
brightest and best.

New Hampshire, U.S.A.

Old Roads and New

We have tramped the old old roads. We know where
each one ends...We know the journey, yard by yard,
the turnings and the bends. We want a bright new
road to take — fresh country to explore — striking out
upon a path where none has gone before.
At this hour of destiny — beneath the troubled skies —
What is this strange track that opens out before our
eyes?   Come, let's take it fearlessly. For much the
world has owed — to men who have not been afraid to
take an unknown road.

The Bulwark

Softly roll the little waves upon the golden sand — As
if they loved to reach and touch this dear and pleasant
land — Curling round the cliffs of Britain, kindly,
tenderly — Breaking in a gentle rhythm... Can this be
the sea — that thundered on the jagged rocks and
broke in clouds of spray — In the wild and bitter fury
of a winter's day. Can this be the sea that tossed the
mighty ships of war — and flung the wreckage of the
storm upon this very shore... Now so placid and so
blue, so peaceful and subdued — It is hard to recollect
that snarling angry mood... Yet for all its changing
ways we Britons love the sea: the bulwark of our island
home, and of our liberty.

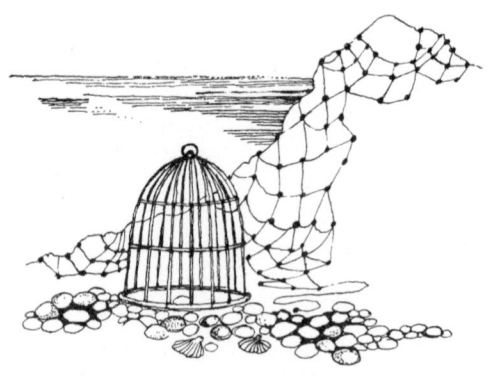

West Dale Bay, Dale, Dyfed, Wales

Too Long

Too long my heart has grieved, too long. I knew it
when I heard the song that rippled from the blackbird's
throat — for with the rapture of that note — there
came a sudden sweet release — and a sense of inner
peace on my wounded spirit stole — bringing healing
to my soul.
Instead of bitterness and pain — my heart remembered
once again — the things that I had thrust away; the
memories of yesterday... I found again my lost belief
— I'd forgotten in my grief — that the world was
beautiful — and that God was merciful.

The Green Wave

A wave of green has broken on the April countryside
— sweeping round the woods and hedges like a rising
tide... A mounting wave of living green goes rolling
round the world — as on twig and branch and bough
the new leaves are uncurled.
Lovely at this season is the flowering cherry tree — like
a white-sailed galleon upon a restless sea — a ship
adrift before the wind; a fair and graceful thing —
riding on the full green waters of the tides of Spring.

Forest Tapestry

In Spring the leafing woods are like a finely woven
tapestry — Every shade of green is worked into the
canvas, for we see — larch and lime and ash and hazel,
birch and beeches, fresh and bright — with their
thickly tangled branches caught in webs of amber
light.
Here and there the deep dark tones of pine and fir and
sombre yew — are flecked with dazzling streaks of
colour where the shining sky breaks through... And all
around the forest edge the gorse-clad common can be
seen — framing it in burning beauty... weaving gold
into the green.

In a Country Churchyard

In the kindly shelter of a widely spreading tree — Lord
and labourer are one in Death's community... Peer
and ploughman come together, stripped and
dispossessed — in the holy acre where the dead are
laid to rest.
One comes from the cottage and the other from the
hall — Christened, wed and buried in the shadow of
this wall... Separated in the world by wealth and blood
and birth — sharing now by equal right a strip of
English earth.

Exeter Cathedral, Exeter, Devonshire, England

The Changing Scene

Here last year the wild flowers made a carpet at our feet — Buttercup and pimpernel, vetch, poppy, marguerite... The fields were flushed with sorrel and the bracken stood waist high — where the heathered hills flowed out to meet the distant sky. Now it's all been ploughed and there's a different kind of scene — Miles of furrowed earth where once were meadows gay and green: long straight lines of growing crops in patterns trim and neat — and soon the rolling acres will be bright with ripened wheat.

Let Not the Vision Fade

It is all too easy a backward step to take — To sever
links of friendship and promises to break...To shatter
things of value in a rebellious mood — Forgetting
obligations and debts of gratitude.
O Let us then remember the perils we have shared; the
price we paid for freedom; the dangers we have dared.
The fellowships of battle; the sacrifices made. Let not
the glory vanish! Let not the vision fade!

Poppies, Calais, France

Mosaic

From this window in the hills the valley can be seen —
a rich and beautiful mosaic, mauve and brown and
green; meres and meadows, roads and hedges in a
pattern laid — Like tessellated pavement, wonderfully
made.
Little squares of palest gold where wheat and barley
grow. Emerald pastures veined with silver where the
brooklets flow. Hayfields with their yellow ricks; dark
woods of beech and oak. Red-roofed hamlets hazy
with the blue of cottage smoke.

Beddgelert, Gwynedd, Wales

Ever Grateful

I recall that first strange meeting. Surely it was Fate.
Fortune smiled upon me then. It was my lucky date.
Having you, I've got the world: life's sweetest, and
life's best. Ever grateful I should feel to be so richly
blessed.

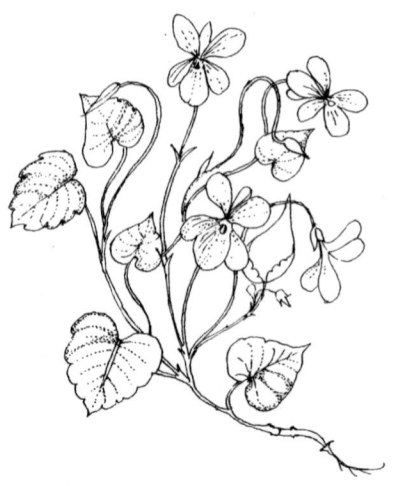

Cader Idris, Arthog, Barmouth, Gwynedd, Wales

Lonely Heart

Lost love, dear love, come to me in dreams. Stretch
your arms across the gulf of Death. Fill the silences of
solitude. Speak through birdsong, and the wind's
warm breath.
Lost love, dear love, lodge within my heart. Turn my
doubts into a faith sublime. Change my sorrow into
secret bliss. Walk beside me to the end of time.

When Came the Great Calamity

When came the great calamity — We knew where our
salvation lay. The nation at the King's Command —
paused from its work, to kneel and pray.
When came the great catastrophe — We called aloud
upon His name — and in manner wonderful — The cry
was heard. The answer came. To generations yet
unborn — these things declare with prayer and praise.
Let our children's children know the story of those
glorious days.

Duncansby Head, Caithness-shire, Scotland

Remember and be Faithful

Keep your love untarnished... Be staunch and straight
and true. Be loyal... and betray not the one who trusts
in you. No fleeting hour of pleasure is worth a life's
regret. Be strong, though great temptations around
your path are set. Happiness is precious.
... Too precious to destroy. Folly leads to sorrow and
virtue leads to joy... Self-respect is sweeter than any
passing smile. Remember and be faithful...Remember
all the while.

Rose with Primula

An Old Cottage

There's a certain charm about a cottage quaint and old
— a warm and human sort of feeling, for it seems to
hold — something of the life of all the souls who long
ago — lived and worked and dreamed their dreams
beside the hearth's bright glow.
Houses that are newly built can never re-create — just
this sort of atmosphere, so snug and intimate...
Roofed with moss-encrusted tiles or thatched with
reed and rush — Beamed with oak and walled with
stones that catch the sun's gold flush.
Nowhere else but in a little cottage can you find — this
enfolding cosiness that brings to heart and mind —
deep contentment and the boon of quiet happiness.
Rich you are indeed if such a cottage you possess.

Cottage in Sussex, England

88

The Lessons of Misfortune

It's easy to be grateful for life's good and happy days
— to lift the heart in joyous prayer of thankfulness and
praise — when everything is going well with not a
cloud in view — when all the roads run smoothly and
our dreams are coming true.
But we must learn to thank God for the things that
bring us low — If we never had to fight, the soul would
never grow... That which wounds the vanity and
curbs the selfish will — is an opportunity for wresting
good from ill.

Dahlias

Worst or Best

It's the little things of life that make it all worthwhile:
the gracious gesture quietly made, the unexpected
smile — The courteous act, the kindly thought... the
little things that can't be bought.
It's the little things of life that prove just what we are
— What we say can charm and please or it can hurt
and jar... It's the little things that test — and show us
at our worst or best.

Do Not Fret

Do not fret and worry over things you cannot change
— What's the use of beating at a wall? ... When you
know that the solution lies beyond your range —
worrying will do no good at all. Do not wear away your
strength in futile questionings — for perhaps you'll
need it by and by ... Do not waste your energy, but
keep it for the things — you can alter if you really try.